Bugs

Guided/Group Reading Notes

Blue Band

Contents

OXFORD

Introduction

Reading progression in Year I/Primary 2

Year I/Primary 2 is a period of rapid development in reading for most children as they move from being enthusiastic beginning readers to becoming confident early readers. Pleasure in reading is promoted through the teacher reading aloud to the children a wide range of stories, poems, rhymes and information texts. Children experience a range of fiction, non-fiction, poetry and other texts during shared, guided and independent reading. Ample opportunities are given for the children to discuss texts, select their own texts and use information texts purposefully. This helps children to develop as self-motivated, enthusiastic readers who recognize the point of reading and are beginning to develop their own interests and preferences in reading.

Children are supported to read independently using short texts containing a core of familiar and decodable words. By the end of Year I/P2, most children recognize an increasing number of high frequency words automatically. They apply their phonic knowledge when trying to read and write more complex and unfamiliar words. The children also use context and syntax to check that what they are reading makes sense. Pictures are used to support the children's understanding of the text and to gain additional information not stated in the text. As their reading skills develop, they self-correct more rapidly, often demonstrating that they are monitoring meaning as they read. Their reading fluency develops as they listen to models of fluent, expressive reading, pay attention to basic punctuation, use their store of automatically recognized words and reread and re-visit texts.

Project X and progression in phonics

The primary approach to teaching children to read is through systematic synthetic phonics and the Project X books fully support this approach, whilst also providing children with rich and engaging reading experiences.

The Project X books at **blue band** are closely aligned to Phase 4 of *Letters and Sounds*. They support the consolidation of learning from Phases 2 and 3 and extend children's blending skills by introducing longer words, adjacent consonants, multi-syllable and compound words. The texts offer children frequent opportunities to apply their developing phonic skills to reading decodable words and 'tricky' high-frequency words such as **said**, **what** and **like**. The remaining language is appropriately levelled to draw on children's natural speech patterns and familiar vocabulary, and acts as a valuable stimulus for talk and comprehension.

A chart showing the alignment of all titles at blue band to the phonic progression in *Letters and Sounds* is provided in the *Teaching Handbook* for Year 1/P2. Details of the decodable and other vocabulary in each book in the **Bugs** cluster is given on pages 10-11 of these *Guided/Group Reading Notes*.

At **blue band** children's reading development is further supported by predictable events, natural language patterns, rhyme and rhythm, and repeated words, phrases and sentences. Longer sentences and a variety of sentence structures are also introduced. The stories in each cluster all have a clear beginning, middle and end, to support children's growing understanding of story structure. The non-fiction books contain an increasing number of non-fiction features such as contents pages, labelled diagrams, headings, simple questions and captions.

Progression in the Project X character books

In this cluster, we continue to get to know the core characters and their families. The friends continue to use the shrinking powers of their watches. In *Ant's Bug Adventure*, Ant finds out what it is like to be confronted by a 'huge' stag beetle. In *The Race*, Tiger and Cat race each other – Tiger in a super buggy, Cat on a snail. The events mirror the story of the 'The Hare and the Tortoise' and Cat wins through with her steady determination.

The shrinking power of the watches is simply a given a this stage. In later books the full potential of the watches is revealed and readers discover where they come from.

Guided/Group Reading

The engaging content and careful levelling of Project X books makes them ideal for use in guided/group reading sessions. The advantages of guided/group reading are discussed in the *Teaching Handbook* for Year 1/P2. The handbook also contains a chart showing the approximate reading level for each colour band.

To use the books in guided/group reading sessions, you should select a band that creates a small degree of challenge for the group of pupils. Typically they should be able to read about 90% of the book unaided. This level of 'readability' provides the context for children to practise their reading and build reading confidence. The 'challenge' in the text provides opportunities for explicitly teaching reading skills.

These *Guided/Group Reading Notes* provide support for each book in the **Bugs** cluster, along with suggestions for follow-up activities.

Speaking, listening and drama

Talk is crucial to learning. Children need plenty of opportunities to express their ideas through talk and drama, and to listen to and watch the ideas of others. These processes are important for building reading engagement, personal response and understanding. Suggestions for speaking, listening and drama are given for every book.

Discussion around a text is important for developing understanding and engagement. Advice on promoting discussion and comprehension through the use of 'open' questions and techniques for encouraging extended dialogue, are given in the *Teaching Handbook* for Year 1/P2. Within these *Guided/Group Reading Notes* the speaking and listening activities are linked to the reading assessment focuses.

Building comprehension

Understanding what we have read is at the heart of reading and is central to children's motivation. Comprehension is not something to be left until decoding skills are established. It should be encouraged from children's earliest encounters with print. The crucial concept that print carries meaning is what gives purpose to the act of reading. Children who get pleasure from being read to and from reading are more likely to become engaged and enthusiastic readers. Enjoyment and seeing a purpose to reading helps children, especially boys, remain motivated and eager to learn.

To help beginning readers understand a text, these *Guided/Group Reading Notes* contain practical strategies to develop the following important aspects of comprehension:

- Previewing
- Predicting
- Activating and building prior knowledge
- Questioning
- Recall
- Visualizing and other sensory responses
- Deducing, inferring and drawing conclusions
- Determining importance
- Synthesizing
- Empathizing
- Summarizing
- Personal response, including adopting a critical stance.

Over time activities that cover all these aspects of comprehension are introduced. The research basis and rationale for these aspects of comprehension is given in the *Teaching Handbook* for Year I/P2.

Building vocabulary

Explicit work on enriching vocabulary is important in building reading fluency and comprehension. Repeatedly encountering a word and its variants helps it become known on sight. The thematic 'cluster' structure of Project X supports this because words are repeated within and across books. Suggestions for vocabulary work are included in these *Guided/Group Reading*

Notes. The vocabulary chart on pages 10–11 shows when vocabulary is repeated and new words introduced. It also indicates those words that can be used in a structured phonics and spelling programme.

Reading fluency

Reading fluency combines automatic word recognition and reading with pace and expression. Rereading, fluency and building comprehension support each other. This is discussed more fully in the *Teaching Handbook* for Year 1/P2. Opportunities for children to read aloud are important in building fluency and reading aloud to children provides models of expressive fluent reading. Suggestions for purposeful and enjoyable oral reading and rereading/re-listening activities are given in the follow-up activities in these *Guided/Group Reading Notes* and in the notes for parents on the inside cover of each book.

The Project X *Interactive Stories* software can be used to provide a model of reading fluency for the whole class and/or opportunities for individuals or small groups of children to listen to stories again and again. Listening to stories being read is particularly effective with EAL children. The title, *Ant's Bug Adventure* from this cluster is included on the CD-ROM for Year1/P2.

Developing a thematic approach

Helping children make links in their learning supports their development as learners. All the books in this cluster have a focus on the theme **Bugs**. A chart showing the cross-curricular potential of this theme, and further reading suggestions are given in the *Teaching Handbook* for Year 1/P2, along with a rationale for using thematic approaches. Some suggestions for cross-curricular activities are also given in the follow-up suggestions for each book in these notes.

In guided/group reading sessions, you will also want to encourage children to make links between the books in the cluster. Grouping books in a cluster allows readers to make links between characters, events and actions across the books. This enables readers to gradually build complex understandings of characters, to give reasons why things happen and how characters may change and develop. It can help the children recognize cause and effect. It helps children reflect on the skill of determining importance as a minor incident or detail in one book may prove to have greater significance when considered across several books.

In the **Bugs** cluster, some of the suggested links that can be explored across the books include:

- inventing alliterative phrases for minibeasts (**Literacy**)
- playing snail hopscotch (**Maths**, **PE**)
- classifying insects. (**Science**)

Reading into writing

The character books provide both models and inspiration to support writing. Suggestions for relevant, contextualized and interesting writing activities are given in follow-up activities for each book. These include both short and longer writing opportunities. The activities cover a wide range of writing contexts so writers can develop an understanding of adapting their writing for different audiences and purposes. The oral activities and role play suggested in these *Guided/Group Reading Notes* also have the potential for extension into writing activities.

The Project X *Interactive Stories* software contains a collection of 'clip art' assets from the character books – characters, setting and props – that children can use in their writing.

Selecting follow-up activities

These *Guided/Group Reading Notes* give many ideas for follow-up activities. Some of these can be completed within the guided/group reading session. Some are longer activities that will need to be worked on over time. You should select those activities that are most appropriate for your class. It is not expected that you would complete all the suggested activities.

Home/school reading

Parents are vital partners in developing children's reading enjoyment, confidence and enthusiasm. Books used in a guided/group reading session can also be used in home/school reading programmes.

Following a guided/group reading session, the child could:
- reread the book at home to build reading confidence and fluency
  - read a related book from the cluster.

    Notes and ideas for parents on supporting their child in reading at home is provided in the inside covers of individual books. Further advice for teachers concerning home/school reading partnerships is given in the *Teaching Handbook* for Year 1/P2.

Assessment

During guided/group reading teachers make ongoing assessments of individuals and of the group. Reading targets are indicated for each book and you should assess against these. Select just one or two targets at a time as the focus for the group. The same target can be appropriate for several literacy sessions or over several texts. Readers should be encouraged to self-assess and peer-assess against the target/s.

Further support for assessing pupils' progress is provided in the *Teaching Handbook* for Year 1/P2.

Continuous reading objectives and ongoing assessment

The following framework objectives will be supported in *every* guided/group reading session and are therefore a *continuous* focus for attention and assessment. They are not repeated in full in each set of notes but as you listen to individual children reading, you should undertake assessment against these decoding and encoding objectives:

- Use syntax and content when reading for meaning **7.2**
- Recognize automatically an increasing number of familiar high frequency words **5.4**
- Apply phonic knowledge and skills as the prime approach to reading and spelling unfamiliar words that are not completely decodable **5.5**
- Read more challenging texts which can be decoded using their acquired phonic knowledge and skills, along with automatic recognition of high frequency words **5.6**

Further objectives are provided as a focus within the notes for each book. Correlation to the specific objectives within the Scottish, Welsh and Northern Ireland curricula are provided in the *Teaching Handbook* for Year 1/P2.

 Recording assessment

The assessment chart for the **Bugs** cluster is provided in the *Teaching Handbook* for Year 1/P2.

 Diagnostic assessment

If an individual child is failing to make good progress or he or she seems to have a specific problem with some aspect of reading you will want to undertake a more detailed assessment. Details of how to use running records for diagnostic assessment are given in the *Teaching Handbook* for Year 1/P2.

📖 Vocabulary chart

The blue band books offer opportunities for children to practise and apply their decoding skills and high frequency word knowledge, develop comprehension, and build their enjoyment of reading. The vocabulary for practising their decoding skills, in line with Phase 4 of *Letters and Sounds* is indicated below, as are the relevant irregular high frequency words.

Young readers widen their vocabulary by encountering new words in the context of a story or information text. The careful levelling in Project X at blue band means that most of the new words children meet will be decodable, but some words may be beyond children's current phonic knowledge even if they are orally familiar – words such as 'happy' or 'play', for example. These are listed as 'challenge' words below. Children should be encouraged to apply their decoding skills to reading these words as far as possible, then helped through the 'tricky' bits of the word or simply told the word so that the flow of their reading isn't disrupted.

The Race	Decodable words (Phase 4)	going, buttons, rocket, ever, never, waiting, winning, snail, sure, fails, grin, with, trees
	Phonic focus: /ai/ /ng/	snail, fails, waiting, winning, going, playing
	Irregular high-frequency words	said, what, do, looked, like, there, so
	Challenge words	race, micro-buggy, idea, secret, dragonfly, day-dreamed, playing, time
Ant's Bug Adventure	Decodable words (Phase 4)	button, faster, pointed, landed, fast, flash, stag, black, jump, help, shook, again
	Phonic focus: adjacent consonants	fast, flash, stag, black, jump, help
	Irregular high-frequency words	said, were, out
	Challenge words	beetle, scary, walk, talk, photo, watch, jaws, inside

Bug Hunt	**Decodable words** (Phase 4)	hunt, look, this, long, help, wing, rest, fast, night, glass, ever, flowers, feelers, earwig,
	Phonic focus: two-syllable words	flowers, feelers, earwig
	Irregular high-frequency words	do, one, what, like, have, about
	Challenge words	ladybird, eight, spider, flies, house, stones, body
Zak and Zee	**Decodable words** (Phase 4)	bigger, green, just, hear, still, tail, small, another
	Phonic focus: /er/ /ear/	ear, hear, bigger, another, wonder
	Irregular high-frequency words	one, were, out, said, do, like, come, some, have, so
	Challenge words	eyes, very, dragonfly, face, flew, play
What Do Bugs Eat?	**Decodable words** (Phase 4)	bigger, into, remember, contents, food, drink, from, plant, fur, jump, rolls, hunt, small
	Phonic focus: adjacent consonants	drink, plant, hunt, small, jump, from
	Irregular high-frequency words	do, what, some, something
	Challenge words	ladybird, spider, aphids, beetle, fleas, locust, blood, bite, eat, water bear, whose

The Race

BY TONY BRADMAN

About this book

Cat and Tiger have a race. Tiger has the micro-buggy but Cat only has a snail. Although Tiger is fast he day-dreams while Cat keeps going. She wins.

You will need

• *Sequencing The Race* Photocopy Master, *Teaching Handbook* for Year 1/P2

	Literacy Framework objective	Target and assessment focus
Decoding and phonics **Phonic focus:** /ai/ /ng/	○ See continuous objectives for decoding and encoding on page 9.	○ We can sound out and blend phonemes all through a word **AF1** ○ We can read words with adjacent consonants **AF1**
Speaking, listening, group interaction and drama	○ Take turns to speak, listen to each other's suggestions ... **3.1**	○ We can talk about what we thought of the story and listen to each other's comments **AF2**
Reading	○ Make predictions showing an understanding of ideas, events and characters **7.3**	○ We can make sensible predictions about what might happen in a story **AF3**

Before reading

To activate prior knowledge and encourage prediction

- Look closely at the picture on the cover. Ask the children what they can see. What are Cat and Tiger doing?

- Read the title. Discuss any ideas the children have about what might happen in the story. (**predicting**)

. . . . >

Assessment point

Can the children make sensible predictions about what might happen in a text? **AF3**

To support decoding skills

- **Phonic opportunity** Draw attention to words with adjacent consonants: *snail*, *fast*, *tree*, *went*, *grin*. Read one of the words, sound it out and demonstrate how to blend the adjacent consonants. Ask the children to take it in turns to identify and blend the separate consonant sounds in one of the other words.

- **Phonic opportunity** Alternatively, depending on the phonic work you have been undertaking, select one or two of the words from the book (see vocabulary chart on page 10) and remind the children how to sound and blend phonemes.

- You may also wish to point out some of the high or medium frequency words or practise decoding some of the phonically regular words in this book and listed in the vocabulary chart on page 10.

*To engage readers, introduce new vocabulary and support
fluent reading*

- Depending on your usual practice and the group you are
  working with, you may wish to:
  - Share the book with the children before they read it
    themselves. Read the first few pages together and ask
    the children to read the rest independently. In this case
    pause after page 5 and ask the children how Cat might
    be feeling when Tiger makes fun of her sled.
    (**empathizing**) Then read pages 6 and 7 to support the
    children with the more challenging vocabulary: *smoke*,
    ready and *steady*. Briefly look at pages 12 and 14 to
    focus on *day-dreamed* and *secret*. Afterwards ask the
    children to read the book independently.
  - Invite the children to read the whole book independently.

 During reading

- Ask the children to read the book quietly.
- If you have not already done so, ask the children what
  to do if they encounter a difficult word, modelling with
  an example from the book if necessary. Remind the
  children of the more challenging vocabulary which you
  looked at before reading the book. Praise children who
  successfully decode unfamiliar words.
- As you listen to individual children read, you may wish
  to ask some of the following questions to check their
  understanding of the story:
  - What are Cat and Tiger doing? (pp.4–5)
  - Why does Tiger say 'You will only see my
    smoke'? (pp.6–7)
  - What was Tiger day-dreaming about? (p.12)

................................>

> **Assessment point**
>
> Listen to individual
> children reading and
> make ongoing
> assessments on their
> approach to tackling
> new words and their
> reading fluency. **AF1**

After reading

Returning to the text
- Ask the children to take it in turns to tell the group what they thought of the story. Which part did they enjoy most? Why? Encourage the children to respond to each other's comments. (**personal response**)

- >

- Ask the children to tell you briefly what happened in the story. (**recall, summarizing**)
- Ask the children to explain why Tiger thought he would win. (**deducing, inferring**)
- Why do the children think Cat won in the end? (**recall, deducing, inferring, drawing conclusions**)

Building comprehension
- Ask the children to imagine how Tiger felt when he lost the race. Have the children ever lost a race? How did they feel? (**empathizing**)
- Challenge children to order the pictures on the *Sequencing The Race* Photocopy Master and add sentences to them, either orally or in writing. (**summarizing**)

Building vocabulary
- Look back at the text and read some of the pages again, e.g. pages 2–4, 5 and 6, and 12 and 13. What do the children notice about some of the words? (They rhyme, e.g. *do/too*, *joke/smoke*, *grin/win*).

Follow-up activities

Writing activities

- Encourage the children to imagine themselves in the role of Cat. What object and minibeast would the children use to make a 'racing buggy'? Why would they choose that object or minibeast? The children could draw a picture of it and label it. (**short writing task**)

- The children could use some of the pictures from the *Sequencing The Race* Photocopy Master to write part of the story. (**longer writing task**)

Other literacy activities

- Read the story of 'The Hare and the Tortoise' and discuss similarities with this story. (**speaking and listening**)

"This micro-buggy is so fast. You will only see my smoke!"

"Race you to the tree!" said Tiger. "Ready, steady, here we go!"

Cross-curricular and thematic opportunities

- Design/make a 'racing buggy'. (**Art and design, DT**)

- Children could do some research about snails using simple information books or the Internet. They could then write/draw two facts about snails. (**Science**)

- Go on a snail hunt and investigate snail trails. Use a piece of string to 'measure' the snail trails or an egg-timer to time the snails' movements. (**Science**)

- Use thumb prints, potato prints or string to make pictures of snails. (**Art and design**)

- Play snail hopscotch by drawing a huge snail shell with the squares of the hopscotch coiling into the middle and numbered one to ten. Starting at the outside of the shell, throw a small pebble on to the first square, then hop in the square, pick up the pebble and hop out again. Continue this way, right through to the end square, just as if the children were playing an ordinary game of hopscotch. (**Maths, PE**)

Ant's Bug Adventure

BY JAN BURCHETT AND SARA VOGLER

About this book

Ant makes himself small to look inside a log and sees a stag beetle.

You will need

- *Match the picture* Photocopy Master, *Teaching Handbook* for Year I/P2
- *What does Ant think, feel, say?* Photocopy Master, *Teaching Handbook* for Year I/P2
- Pictures of a stag beetle, millipede, ladybird and a snail

	Literacy Framework objective	Target and assessment focus
Decoding and phonics.	○ See continuous objectives for decoding and encoding on page 9.	○ **Phonic focus:** We can read words with adjacent consonants **AF1**
Speaking, listening, group interaction and drama	○ Retell stories, ordering events using story language 1.2	○ We can explain the main events of the story in a clear sequence **AF2**
Reading	○ Visualize and comment on events, characters and ideas, making imaginative links to their own experiences 8.2	○ We can discuss the story and talk about our own similar experiences **AF6**

Before reading

To activate prior knowledge and encourage prediction

- Look closely at the picture on the cover of the book. Ask the children what they can see. What are Ant and his dad doing?

- Read the title. Discuss any ideas of what might happen in this story. (**predicting**)

To support decoding and word recognition

- **Phonic opportunity** Draw attention to words with adjacent consonants: *black, stag, fast, jump, help.* Read one of the words, sound it out and demonstrate how to blend the adjacent consonants. Ask the children to take it in turns to identify and blend the separate consonant sounds in one of the other words.

- **Phonic opportunity** Alternatively, depending on the phonic work you have been undertaking, select one or two of the words from the book (see vocabulary chart on page 10) and remind the children how to sound and blend phonemes.

- You may also wish to point out some of the high or medium frequency words or practise decoding some of the phonically regular words in this book and listed in the vocabulary chart on page 10.

To engage readers, introduce new vocabulary and support fluent reading

- If possible, look at some pictures of minibeasts, e.g. stag beetle, millipede, ladybird, snail. Alternatively, use the pictures from the *Match the picture* Photocopy master. Do the children know the names of the minibeasts? Have the children seen any of these minibeasts before? (**activating prior knowledge**)

- Depending on your usual practice and the group you are working with, you may wish to:
  - Share the book with the children before they read it themselves. Read the first few pages together and ask the children to read the rest independently. In this case, read pages 4 and 5 to the children using expression. Then ask the children to read the book independently.
  - Invite the children to read the whole book independently.

 During reading

- Ask the children to read the book quietly.
- If you have not already done so, ask the children what to do if they encounter a difficult word, modelling with an example from the book if necessary. Remind them of the more challenging vocabulary which you looked at before reading the book. Praise children who successfully decode unfamiliar words.
- As you listen to individual children read, you may wish to ask some of the following questions to check their understanding of the story:
  - What does Ant think? (p.4)
  - Why does he think this? (p.4)
  - What does Ant see in the log? (p.8)
  - Why does Ant point his watch at the stag beetle? (p.12)
  - What does Ant say to the stag beetle? (p.16)

Assessment point

Listen to individual children reading and make ongoing assessments on their decoding approach to tackling new words and their reading fluency.
AF1

After reading

Returning to the text

- Ask the children what they thought of the story. Which part did they enjoy most? Why? (**personal response**)
- Ask the children to tell you briefly what happened in the story. (**recall, summarizing**)

· >

- Can the children explain why Ant was bored? (**deducing, inferring**)
- Encourage the children to discuss how Ant felt when he saw all the bugs. (**deducing, inferring, drawing conclusions, empathizing**)

Building comprehension

- Ask the children to imagine what Ant was thinking and feeling when he was chased by the stag beetle. Use the *What does Ant think, feel, say?* Photocopy Master. How would the children feel if they were chased by the stag beetle? What would they do? (**empathizing, visualizing**)

· >

- Ask one of the children to role play being Ant and invite the other children to ask 'him' questions based on the experiences shown in the book. (**questioning, empathizing**)

Building vocabulary

- Look at page 11 and read the description of the beetle: *The beetle was black with big jaws.* What do the children notice about some of the words? Rearrange the words, e. g. *'big black beetle'* and explain that this is an example of alliteration. Ask the children to talk with a partner to see if, together, they can make up a similar phrase for some other minibeasts (ladybird, ant, spider, snail, millipede).

Suddenly the log shook. Ant saw a big, dark shape. He was amazed. It was a stag beetle.

The beetle was black with big jaws.
"Yikes!" said Ant. "I will use my watch to take a photo."

Follow-up activities

Writing activities

- Using the *Match the picture* Photocopy Master match the silhouette to the picture of the minibeast and write the name of the minibeast. (**short writing task**)

- Write the story on a computer using clip art and speech bubbles. (**longer writing task**)

Other literacy activities

- Watch the story on the Project X *Interactive Stories* software.

Cross-curricular and thematic opportunities

- Children could do some research about stag beetles using simple information books or the Internet. They could then write/draw two facts about stag beetles. (**Science**)
- Create an environment (log pile) to encourage stag beetles and other minibeasts. See: http://www.bbc.co.uk/breathingplaces/doonething/quick/woodpile.shtml (**Science**)
- Make a minibeast collage using paper, scraps of material, etc. (**Art and design**)
- Use clay/modelling materials to make a small sculpture of a minibeast. (**Art and design**)

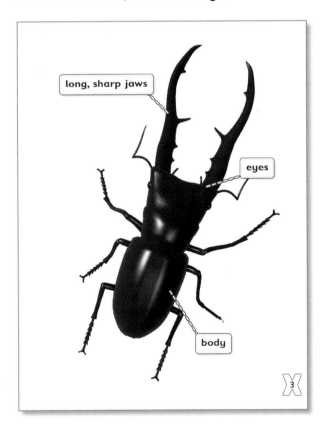

long, sharp jaws

eyes

body

Bug Hunt

BY CLAIRE LLEWELLYN

About this book

Ant goes on a bug hunt in his house and garden. He finds a variety of minibeasts.

You will need

- *Minibeasts quiz* Photocopy Master, *Teaching Handbook* for Year 1/P2
- *Label the minibeasts* Photocopy Master, *Teaching Handbook* for Year 1/P2
- Magnifying glass and pictures of an earwig, ant, a ladybird, fly, moth and spider

	Literacy Framework objective	Target and assessment focus
Decoding and phonics	○ See continuous objectives for decoding and encoding on page 9.	○ **Phonic focus:** We can read two-syllable words: earwig, feelers, flowers **AF1**
Speaking, listening, group interaction and drama	○ Experiment with and build new stores of words to communicate in different contexts 1.4	○ We have understood and used some new words related to minibeasts **AF2**
Reading	○ ... find specific information in simple texts 7.1 ○ Distinguish fiction and non-fiction texts and the different purposes for reading them 8.3	○ We can answer questions by finding the information in books **AF2** ○ We understand what non-fiction books are and why people write and read them **AF4/6**

Before reading

To activate prior knowledge and encourage prediction

- Discuss with the children what they already know about Ant and his character. (**activating prior knowledge**)

- Look at the cover. Ask the children what Ant is doing. What kinds of bugs (minibeasts) do the children think Ant will find? (**predicting**)

To support decoding and word recognition

- **c Phonic opportunity** Draw attention to the two-syllable words in the text: *earwig, feelers, flowers.* Model breaking these longer words down to help with decoding and blending.

- **c Phonic opportunity** Alternatively, depending on the phonic work you have been undertaking, select other decodable words from the book (see vocabulary chart on page 11) and remind the children how to sound and blend phonemes.

- You may also wish to point out some of the high or medium frequency words or practise decoding some of the phonically regular words in this book and listed in the vocabulary chart on page 11.

To engage readers, introduce new vocabulary and support fluent reading

- Look at page 3. What is Ant holding? What is it used for? Demonstrate how a magnifying glass is used. Then look at the pictures of the minibeasts (earwig, ant, ladybird, fly, moth and spider). Can the children name them? Where can these bugs be found? What kind of bugs do the children like? (**activating prior knowledge**)

- Depending on your usual practice and the group you are working with, you may wish to:
  - Share the book with the children before they read it themselves. Model pausing at new vocabulary and checking meaning.
  - Read a few pages together and ask the children to read the rest independently. In this case, read pages 4 and 5 together as these contain some new vocabulary. Then ask the children to read the book independently.
  - Invite the children to read the whole book independently.

 During reading

- Ask the children to read the book quietly.
- If you have not already done so, ask the children what to do if they encounter a difficult word, modelling with an example from the book if necessary. Remind the children of the more challenging vocabulary which you looked at before reading the book. Praise children who successfully decode unfamiliar words.
- As you listen to individual children you may wish to ask some of the following questions to check their understanding of the book:
  - Where did Ant hunt for bugs? (p.3)
  - How many legs does an earwig have?
  - What does it use its feelers for? (p.5)
  - What does Ant say about the fly? (p.10)

....>

> **Assessment point**
>
> Listen to individual children reading and make ongoing assessments on their approach to tackling new words and their reading fluency. **AF1**

After reading

Returning to the text

- Ask the children what they thought of the book and which part they enjoyed most. Why? (**personal response**)

- What is it that shows this is a non-fiction book rather than a story book? Discuss why people read and write non-fiction books and magazines (for information, enjoyment) and ask the children to give you personal examples. You may need to discuss the fictional figure (Ant) and point out he is not involved in a story in this book but is being used for a factual purpose. (**deducing, inferring, drawing conclusions**)

Look on this leaf. What can you see? It is an earwig.

Wow!

·····························>

Building comprehension

- Ask the children:
  - Does Ant like bugs? How do you know?
  - Where did he find the earwig, ant, ladybird, fly, moth and the spider?
  - Why was the moth sleeping? (**recall, deducing, inferring, drawing conclusions**)

·····························>

Assessment point
Can the children discuss what non-fiction books are and why people write and read them? AF4/6

Assessment point
Can the children answer the questions by finding the information in the book? AF2

Building vocabulary

- What are the things called that are on the ant's head? If the children in the group know the word 'antennae', this might be a good opportunity to introduce it as an alternative to feelers.

- Play the *What am I?* game. This could be played in pairs or as a whole group. Model the activity by giving one or two clues about one of the minibeasts, e.g. 'This bug has six legs and two eyes. It likes leaves.' (earwig) The children try to guess which minibeast you are describing.

- Then, ask the children, in pairs, to devise their own clues about a minibeast and invite each pair to say their clues so that the rest of the group can guess the minibeast. (**speaking and listening**)

> **Assessment point**
>
> Have the children understood and used some new words related to minibeasts? **AF2**

Look at these flowers.
What can you see?
It is a ladybird.

8

ladybird

ant

fly

earwig

spider

Why don't you have a bug hunt?
What will you find?

16

Follow-up activities

Writing activities

- Use the *Minibeasts quiz* Photocopy Master. (**longer writing task**)
- Children could complete the *Label the minibeasts* Photocopy Master. (**short writing task**)

Cross-curricular and thematic opportunities

- Go on a minibeast hunt. How many different minibeasts can the children find? Make a graph/pictogram. (**Science, Maths**)
- Build an 'insect': children could design the parts of an insect and then assemble them. (**DT**)
- Sort a set of minibeast pictures. (Children could be given categories or decide their own.) (**Maths, Science**)

Zak and Zee

BY JEANNE WILLIS

About this book

Zee Bug cannot see very well. He meets Zak Bug but doesn't realize he's talking to his back. In the end they both fly off together.

You will need

- *Match the rhyming words* Photocopy Master, *Teaching Handbook* for Year 1/P2
- *Zak and Zee* Photocopy Master, *Teaching Handbook* for Year 1/P2
- Pictures of bugs with eye markings, e.g. butterflies (peacock butterfly, owl butterfly), moths (eyed hawk-moth)

	Literacy Framework objective	Target and assessment focus
Decoding and phonics **Phonic focus:** /er/ /ear/	○ See continuous objectives for decoding and encoding on page 9.	○ We can sound out and blend phonemes all through a word **AF1** ○ We can read words with adjacent consonants **AF1**
Speaking, listening, group interaction and drama	○ Explore familiar themes and characters through improvisation and role play **4.1**	○ We can use role play to explore the story **AF2**
Reading	○ Make predictions showing an understanding of ideas, events and characters **7.3**	○ We can make sensible predictions about what might happen in a story **AF3**

Before reading

To activate prior knowledge and encourage prediction

- Look at the cover together, reading the title and the back cover blurb and looking closely at the pictures. What can the children see? What do the children think is going to happen in the story? (**activating prior knowledge, predicting**)

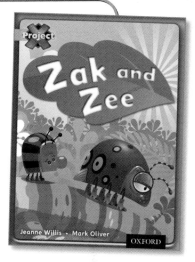

· ·>

To support decoding skills

- **Phonic opportunity** Draw attention to words with adjacent consonants: *green, tree, just, still, small*. Read one of the words, sound it out and demonstrate how to blend the adjacent consonants. Ask the children to take it in turns to identify and blend the separate consonant sounds in one of the other words.

- **Phonic opportunity** Alternatively, depending on the phonic work you have been undertaking, select one or two of the words from the book (see vocabulary chart on page 11) and remind the children how to sound and blend phonemes.

- You may also wish to point out some of the high or medium frequency words or practise decoding some of the phonically regular words in this book and listed in the vocabulary chart on page 11.

To engage readers, introduce new vocabulary and support fluent reading

- Look at pages 2 and 3. Ask the children to describe the two bugs. What is special about Zak Bug? Why does he have 'eye' markings on his back? If possible, show the children some pictures of other insects that have 'eye' markings, e.g. peacock butterfly, eyed hawk-moth. (**deducing**, **inferring**, **drawing conclusions**)

- Look briefly at pages 4, 5, 6 and 7. Discuss each picture in turn and ask the children what is happening. Introduce the more challenging vocabulary, e.g. *dragonfly's* (p.5), *reply* (p.7).

- Depending on your usual practice and the group you are working with, you may wish to:

  - Share the book with the children before they read it themselves.

  - Read the first few pages together and then ask the children to read the rest independently. In this case, read pages 4–7 with the children. What do the children notice about some of the words? (uses rhyming text – *tree/Zee*, *eyes/ dragonfly's*, *small/all*, *Hi!/reply*). Ask the children to read on independently.

  - Invite the children to read the whole book independently.

 During reading

- Ask the children to read the book quietly.

- If you have not already done so, ask the children what to do if they encounter a difficult word, modelling with an example from the book if necessary. Remind the children of the more challenging vocabulary which you looked at before reading the book. Praise children who successfully decode unfamiliar words.

> **Assessment point**
>
> Listen to individual children reading and make ongoing assessments on their approach to tackling new words and their reading fluency. AF1

- As you listen to individual children read, you may wish to ask might want to ask them to stop and summarize what has happened so far and predict what will happen next. (**Summarizing, predicting**)

 After reading

Returning to the text
- Ask the children what they thought of the story and the ending. (**personal response**)
- Ask the children to tell you briefly what happened in the story. (**recall, summarizing**)

Building comprehension
- Ask the children why Zee talked to Zak's back. (**deducing, inferring, drawing conclusions**)
- Discuss how Zee felt when he found out that he had been talking to Zak's back. (**empathizing**)
- Have the children ever felt as if someone has ignored them? How did they feel?
- Ask one of the children to role play being Zee Bug and ask the other children to ask 'him' questions based on the experiences shown in the book. (**questioning, empathizing**)

· ·>

> **Assessment point**
>
> Can children use role play to help them to understand the story? Can they ask and answer relevant questions? **AF2**

Follow-up activities

Writing activities

- Complete the *Match the rhyming words* Photocopy Master. (**short writing task**)
- Invite the children to write another story about Zak and Zee using the *Zak and Zee* Photocopy Master. (**longer writing task**)

Other literacy activities

- Challenge the children to tell the story from Zee's viewpoint. (**speaking and listening**)

Cross-curricular and thematic opportunities

- Make finger puppets of Zee and Zak and role play the story. (**Art and design**)
- Find out more about insects that have 'eye' markings, e.g. peacock butterfly, eyed hawk-moth. (**Science**)
- Collect information about eye colour of children in the class. Produce a block graph or pictogram. (**Maths**)
- Investigate the importance of eyes (linking this to work on senses). (**Science**)

In this story

Zak Bug

Zee Bug

What Do Bugs Eat?

BY HAYDN MIDDLETON

About this book

This non-fiction text looks at a variety of bugs (minibeasts) and what they eat.

You will need

- *Match the bug to its food* Photocopy Master, *Teaching Handbook* for Year 1/P2
- *My favourite bug* Photocopy Master, *Teaching Handbook* for Year 1/P2

	Literacy Framework objective	Target and assessment focus
Decoding and phonics	See continuous objectives for decoding and encoding on page 9.	○ **Phonic focus:** We can read words with adjacent consonants **AF1**
Speaking, listening, group interaction and drama	○ Experiment with and build new stores of words to communicate in different contexts 1.4	○ We have understood and used some new words related to minibeasts **AF2**
Reading	○ Distinguish fiction and non-fiction texts and the different purposes for reading them 8.3	○ We understand what non-fiction books are and why people write and read them **AF4/6**
	○ Find specific informaiton in simple texts 7.1	○ We can answer questions by finding the information in books **AF2**

Before reading

*To activate prior knowledge and
encourage prediction*

- Look at the cover of the book. Ask the
children if they can guess what the bug is.
Together, read the title and the back cover
blurb. What is the book about? Do the
children have any ideas about how a
small bug could eat a bigger bug?
(**activating prior knowledge, predicting**)

To support decoding skills

- **ⓓPhonic opportunity** Draw attention to
words with adjacent consonants: *hunt, jump,
from, drink, plant*. Read one of the words, sound it out and
demonstrate how to blend the adjacent consonants. Ask the
children to take it in turns to identify and blend the separate
consonant sounds in one of the other words.

- **ⓓPhonic opportunity** Alternatively, depending on the phonic
work you have been undertaking, select one or two of the
words from the book (see vocabulary chart on page 11) and
remind the children how to sound and blend phonemes.

- You may also wish to point out some of the high or medium
frequency words or practise decoding some of the phonically
regular words in this book and listed in the vocabulary chart
on page 11.

*To engage readers, introduce new vocabulary
and support fluent reading*

- Read the contents page. How do we use a contents page?
Ask the children to tell you the page where they can find
information about the water bear (p.10) and the dung
beetle (p.12).

- Look briefly at pages 4, 8, 9 and 13. Discuss each picture in
turn and read the text, focusing on the more challenging
vocabulary: *spider* (p.4), *fleas* (p.8), *blood* (p.8), *locust,
team* (p.15).

- Depending on your usual practice and the group you are working with, you may wish to:
  - Share the book with the children before they read it themselves.
  - Read the opening pages together and ask the children to read the rest independently.
  - Invite the children to read the whole book independently.

 ## During reading

- Ask the children to read the book quietly.
- If you have not already done so, ask the children what to do if they encounter a difficult word, modelling with an example from the book if necessary. Remind the children of the more challenging vocabulary which you looked at before reading the book.
- As you listen to individual children read, you may wish to ask some of the following questions to check their understanding of the book:
  - How does the spider capture the fly? (p.4)
  - What do fleas drink? (pp.8–9)
  - How big is a water bear? (p.10)
  - What does a dung beetle eat? What is dung? (p.13)

....>

Assessment point

Listen to individual children reading and make ongoing assessments on their approach to tackling new words and their reading fluency. **AF1**

After reading

Returning to the text

- Ask the children what they thought of the book and which were the most interesting pages. (**personal response**)

- What tells the children that this book is a non-fiction book rather than a story book? Discuss why people read and write non-fiction books and magazines (information, enjoyment). What would people learn from reading this book? (**deducing, inferring, drawing conclusions**)

Assessment point

Can the children discuss what non-fiction books are and why people write and read them? AF4/6

Building comprehension

- Look at pages 10 and 11 together. Ask the children why these minibeasts are called 'water bears'. (**inferring, deducing**)

- What do scientists have to use to be able to see the bugs?

- Read pages 14 and 15. How do the ants manage to eat a bigger bug?

- Look at page 16. Can the children match each bug to what it eats? (**recall**)

- Which is the children's favourite bug in the book? Why? (**personal response**)

Assessment point

Can the children answer questions by finding the information in the book? AF2

Follow-up activities

Writing activities

- Ask the children to match the minibeast to the food it eats, using the *Match the bug to its food* Photocopy Master. (**short writing task**)

- Children could write about their favourite minibeast from the book. Why do the children like this creature? What does it eat? Can the children find out one more fact about their minibeast and write it in the 'Did you know?' box on the *My favourite bug* Photocopy Master? (**longer writing task**)

Cross-curricular and thematic opportunities

- Sort and classify the different bugs/minibeasts. How many legs do they have? Do they have wings? What do they eat? Where do they live? (**Science, Maths**)

- Children could paint or make one of the minibeasts, e.g. ladybird, water bear, dung beetle, flea. (**Art and design, DT**)

Flea

flea

cat

This cat has fleas on its fur.
The fleas will bite the cat.
Then they drink its blood.

Fleas can jump on to you.
Then they drink *your* blood.